Animals
That Live in the
Forest

Porcupines

by JoAnn Early Macken

**Reading consultant: Susan Nations, M.Ed.,
author/literacy coach/consultant**

Gareth Stevens
PUBLISHING

Please visit our website, www.garethstevens.com. For a free color catalog of all our high-quality books, call toll free 1-800-542-2595 or fax 1-877-542-2596.

Library of Congress Cataloging-in-Publication Data

Macken, JoAnn Early, 1953–
    Porcupines / JoAnn Early Macken.
        p. cm. — (Animals that live in the forest)
    Includes bibliographical references and index.
    ISBN-10: 0-8368-4485-8   ISBN-13: 978-0-8368-4485-6 (lib. bdg.)
    ISBN-10: 0-8368-4492-0   ISBN-13: 978-0-8368-4492-4 (softcover)
    1. Porcupines—Juvenile literature.   I. Title.
    QL737.R652M24   2005
    599.35'97—dc22   2004057215

This edition first published in 2005 by
Gareth Stevens Publishing
111 East 14th Street, Suite 349
New York, NY 10003

Art direction: Tammy West
Cover design and page layout: Kami Strunsee
Picture research: Diane Laska-Swanke

Picture credits: Cover, © Joe McDonald/Visuals Unlimited;
p. 5 © Alan & Sandy Carey; p. 7 © Lisa & Mike Husar/TeamHusar.com;
pp. 9, 17 © Tom and Pat Leeson; p. 11 © Lynn M. Stone; pp. 13, 21
© Michael H. Francis; p. 15 © Joe McDonald/Visuals Unlimited; p. 19
© David Cavagnaro/Visuals Unlimited

Printed in the United States of America

4 5 6 7 8 9 10 09 08 07

Note to Educators and Parents

Reading is such an exciting adventure for young children! They are beginning to integrate their oral language skills with written language. To encourage children along the path to early literacy, books must be colorful, engaging, and interesting; they should invite the young reader to explore both the print and the pictures.

Animals That Live in the Forest is a new series designed to help children read about forest creatures. Each book describes a different forest animal's life cycle, eating habits, home, and behavior.

Each book is specially designed to support the young reader in the reading process. The familiar topics are appealing to young children and invite them to read — and re-read — again and again. The full-color photographs and enhanced text further support the student during the reading process.

In addition to serving as wonderful picture books in schools, libraries, homes, and other places where children learn to love reading, these books are specifically intended to be read within an instructional guided reading group. This small group setting allows beginning readers to work with a fluent adult model as they make meaning from the text. After children develop fluency with the text and content, the book can be read independently. Children and adults alike will find these books supportive, engaging, and fun!

— Susan Nations, M.Ed., author, literacy coach, and consultant in literacy development

A baby porcupine is born in spring. Its eyes are open. It has hair and teeth. In less than an hour, it can walk.

The baby, called a **porcupette**, drinks milk from its mother. In a few days, it can climb up a tree. Its sharp claws help it climb.

In a few weeks, it eats grass and other plants. By fall, a young porcupine is ready to be on its own.

Porcupines find their food by its smell. They eat tree bark, twigs, and leaves. Their sharp front teeth keep growing. Chewing keeps them from growing too long.

Porcupines eat mainly at night. During the day, they sleep. They often sleep in trees.

Porcupines have three layers of hair. The top layer is long. The short bottom layer keeps them warm in winter. The middle layer is hard and sharp. The hard, sharp hairs are called **quills**.

14

An angry porcupine raises its quills. It may make a warning sound. It turns its back. It swings its tail.

If the tail slaps an enemy, the quills come out. They stick in the animal's skin. They hurt!

Porcupines are active in winter, even where snow falls. They may stay up in trees for days. Porcupines are at home in the forest.

Glossary

porcupette — a baby porcupine

quills — hard, sharp hairs

layers — **levels that lie over or under each other**

For More Information

Books

Porcupines. Lola M. Schaefer (Heinemann)

Porcupines. Welcome to the World of Animals (series). Diane Swanson (Gareth Stevens)

Prickly and Smooth. Animal Opposites (series). Rod Theodorou and Carole Telford (Heinemann)

Prickly Porcupines. Pull Ahead Books (series). Shannon Zemlicka (Lerner)

Web Site

Natureworks: Common Porcupine
www.nhptv.org/natureworks/porcupine.htm
Porcupine facts and pictures

23

Index

About the Author

JoAnn Early Macken is the author of two rhyming picture books, *Sing-Along Song* and *Cats on Judy*, and six other series of nonfiction books for beginning readers. Her poems have appeared in several children's magazines. A graduate of the M.F.A. in Writing for Children and Young Adults program at Vermont College, she lives in Wisconsin with her husband and their two sons. Visit her Web site at www.joannmacken.com.